69 Ways to Turn Him on In and Out of Bed

ISBN:
978-0-692-87263-5

Cover Designed by AndiPaige Calloway

Printed in the United States of America

Calloway Publishing

ISBN:
978-0-692-8726[illegible]

[illegible] Edited by [illegible]

[illegible] Publishing

For the woman who has everything

69 Ways to Turn Him On In and Out of Bed

Sonia Calloway

Dedication

To Ansel Myles, The man who treats me the way a woman should be treated and the best man I've ever had. Thank you so much for being the man that pushed me to get my work out there for the world to read.

And

To Frank "Maine" Moore, my best friend of 30 years, we never missed a beat.

Acknowledgements

Thanks to my parents for having me and giving me a great life. The two of you always made me feel like I could do anything I wanted.

I'd like to thank all the men that completed the survey and for being completely honest. Thank you to the other men who took the time to read my work and for pushing me on. Thanks to my children for not bothering me when I needed to be alone to write. You two have been pushing me for years even when you shrugged at the title. Paige, thank you for a beautiful book cover; you did an awesome job! (andipaigecalloway@gmail.com) Thanks to my special friends, Latonua Jones, Keisha Holt and Javonne Chen, Sheree Paynter, Danielle Belcher and Phyllis Sanders, for being who you are and always there, to listen to me through everything. Thanks to my sisters LaTonja Calloway, Simone Edison and Yolonda Myles for their laughable bed antics and for telling me to just do the damn thang. Thank you to my two brothers, Tony for keeping my car in tip-top shape to get me every place I need to go to do what I had to do. Thank you Cha, for telling me I could always do everything I put me mind to and having great faith in my abilities. Lorna Bogues and Ansel Myles, thank you for the many hours of editing and proofreading, at times I know it wasn't easy.

Table of Contents

Opening Words From the Author, Ooh, That's Me

"I couldn't suck a dick right even if my life depended on it." Does that sound like something you've said before or have heard your friends say something similar? Well, you're not alone and you're definitely not the worst believe me. Many times we go to the bookstore looking for something, anything to spice up our sex life. The problem is we have to read too much to get to the good parts. I don't know about you, but I just want to know what I have to do and get to it. I don't want to have to read over two hundred pages of boring literature and go through so much medical and sexual terminology that by the time I'm done reading, I'm too tired to perform. This book, just like a lot of other books, might not be for you, but who's to say that's not something someone else is looking for. We all have different things that we're looking for in a relationship, but the one thing we all have in common that we're looking for is total satisfaction between both partners, our own personal freak.

I've tried to make this as easy and simple as possible with the least amount of reading. If you have to read a little bit, I promise it will be short and interesting. Now, just like everything else, you may love everything you read, you may love all 69 ways or you may be one of those people that are so picky that only a few will meet your needs. But that's not what matters when you're reading this book. All that matters is that you find out what you like, then try them on your man. After you've tried all the ways YOU like give him the book and let him highlight the ones he likes. In that way, you can see how much of a freak he's got in him. You may or may not be surprised by the things he picks out, but I guarantee you'll have fun. When you're having fun, it opens up so many avenues to more pleasure. When pleasure is being experienced and is totally accepted, it creates a sense of closeness between both partners. When you feel closer than close to someone and you feel completely safe with him or her, everything seems so much more exciting and unrestricted. You'll feel at ease and you're willing to learn more about each other and even more about your body parts. You'll learn different little things to make his toes curl and what you need to do to keep it flowing smoothly between the two of you. You'll pick up interesting tidbits about simple things that'll make a big difference in your sex life.

I don't claim that this book will make you have an A+ relationship, but communication is the key to a successful relationship. I'm not saying this book will keep your man from cheating, but it doesn't hurt to know all you need to know about sexually stimulating a man. (Besides, if your man is going to cheat, it's his nature or that's how you got him, really, honestly, what do you really expect?) Most men who cheat, usually do something with the other woman that he might not be getting from his mate. Some men want to keep their wives or girlfriends on the angel side, and when he gets a woman on the outside, he may have things done to him he feels his wife or girlfriend is too good to do or perform. Not knowing that you, his wife, his girlfriend might like doing those same things as well. I'm not saying this book will make you the best freak this side of the Mississippi river but you'll be well on your way. What I am claiming is, this book will make you have a lot of fun, and you'll learn so much more about your man's body and the different things he likes. What's even better is that these things can be done in and out of bed.

Communication is the Foundation of Any Successful Relationship

How much do you share with the men you love or date? How soon do you share what's deep inside you? Are you so comfortable with yourself that you can tell a man anything about yourself and still feel all right? Or do you just tell him what you want him to know and feel, sticking with the old line, "What he doesn't know won't hurt him." As a woman, I know what it feels like to give and show a man my soul, only to have him turn it around and use it against me. For that reason, I tell men what I want them to know and what I know they need to hear. If he gains my trust and I his, I don't mind sharing more. Communication is very important in any successful relationship. People have to open up and let one another know what they like, what they feel and what they'd like to feel. Sometimes as women we open up about our personal lives (to men we just meet or have been dating for a short time) and tell him what another guy did to us, or our money matters, but we don't open up as easily to reveal our sexual desires or to help him explore his. Men get so confused by the signals we send; they need to hear from our mouths what we want. If you don't want him to stray like a wild dog, you'd better tell him what you want and be ready to experience all sort of fun nasty stuff. Don't forget to let him know what he's doing to you makes you feel wild and crazy and you want him to do whatever he wants to do with you.

As a woman, I often wonder what other or most women think as far as the role they should play in the relationship. How active should her role be in expressing her wishes and desire when it comes to sex and romance in the relationship? Your role is just as important as his, at least 50 percent as important. If there's something you'd like, you should tell him especially if it makes a big difference in the way you feel about your relationship. After lovemaking, if you want him to hold you 'cause it gives you a sense of security and completeness, tell him. You know most men are roll-over dummies, when they have orgasms, so it just might be necessary for you to coach him into hugging and holding you when you've finished. You shouldn't have to be afraid to say what you're feeling or what you want to feel, if you're in a relationship where the satisfaction of both partners is important. Though you may not like some of the things he likes and vice versa, you still have to respect his desires.

It would be an ideal world, if we could tell our mate all the things we want and desire no matter how nasty or crazy they might be. When it's all said and done, the lines of communication are still open, and no one has any funny feelings. You should be able to tell him, "I love you so much; I just want to fall asleep with your dick in my mouth like a pacifier." In a perfect world, he would be more than happy to let you fall asleep between his legs, keeping him warm in your mouth but that isn't reality and some men would find that appalling, humph! I don't know why. I would love to fall asleep with my man nibbling on my jewel. The way the world is today most people approach the opposite sex with so much caution it makes it almost impossible to relax and open up the way we'd like. Wouldn't it be refreshing to meet a new partner, where you could be the real you, even if you do have whorish tendencies in the bedroom? All of us women have a little freak in us. Some of us just have more than others. It just takes the right man to bring it out.

By talking with and interviewing several men from different backgrounds, they've expressed some different but many similar attitudes when it comes to openness in expressing their desires. Most of them agree that the longer they're in a relationship with a woman, the more intimate they become. Others felt it was important to be intimate from the beginning, so that the feeling of trust, understanding, and acceptance are established.

"I prefer women that I fuck to fuck me like it's their last time fucking. Act like the world is about to end and give me everything you got."

Joseph, Cartoonist, 49

"I love a woman to let me take control in the beginning but as we get to know each other I expect her to grab me by my dick when I walk in the door and tell me she's gotta have it."

Brad, Information Tech, 21

"I just want her to be a hoe in da bedroom and tell me how much she wants me to blow her back out." He laughed right after the comment like he got a kick out of himself. *"I'll blow her back way da fuck out."*

Dylan, Construction Worker, 36

"I like a woman to be aggressive but I don't like it if she makes it look and feel nasty."

Samuel, Engineer, 31

"I love being intimate and romantic especially when I'm first getting with women but it seems they look at me like I'm a wussy *if I want to cuddle so I treat most of them the same, I just fuck them good and send them on their way."*

Hugh, Psychology Major, 20

See what I mean. They all want different things so how do you approach your man or that new guy you have your eye on? The best thing is to be yourself and let him know a little bit at a time while still getting some of the things you want. Some men feel women that are overly aggressive will have problems because the man might think she's like this with every other man she's been with. He wants a hoe in the bedroom not outside of the bedroom. At the same time, they want a woman to be intimate, but not intimate too quickly. If the woman exposes too much of herself, a man will think she's trying to establish something a little more than what's there.

When it comes to women, most men suggest that you get to know them without asking too many questions. They already think we're too nosey as it is, so don't give him a reason to believe the truth. Tell him some things about yourself that will make him feel comfortable enough to do the same with you. If he's feeling comfortable with you, he'll reveal more, and the more he reveals the less you have to ask. When it comes to his deepest feelings, he won't talk about it too easily or too quickly. Don't keep asking him questions for which he's not willing or ready to. When he's ready, he will share He'll open up when he feels you've earned his trust. The more a man learns to understand women, he realizes that with each woman, he can learn a little more. There are things men do know about women, but play stupid in order to give us a false sense of relationship power. Now men know all too well that women can be pleased by the simplest things, besides, what's more simple than a man acting like he doesn't know everything about women but he'd like to know all about us and what makes us feel good. Once he's got you believing that it's all about you, you will be willing to open up and express more.

What Do Men Really Want?

"I'm one of those sensitive guys and I like a lot of body contact. I know a lot of guys don't generally like a woman all over them unless it's during sex but I love when a woman lays on top of me and rubs her body against mines, It could be with or without clothes, it's just the way she starts breathing and I can feel the heat from her body. When I feel that heat I know she's feelin' me."

Ed, Professor, 54

"I like to say whatever's on my mind when it comes to sex. Most guys won't say what they want because they're afraid that the woman will think they're a pervert or is disrespecting them in some form or fashion. Maaan, you can say the wrong thing and it's over just like that!"

Neil, Reporter, 28

"I like when a woman bosses me around. I don't mean like she wants to kick my ass or something but by telling me I better give her what she wants and The way she wants it but she's got to stay a woman." He laughs. "I mean I like it when she says it sexy."

Jeff, Medical Student, 25

"I love when a woman talks dirty and when things are getting' hot I want to know all she's thinking and feelin' and I want to hear sounds letting' me know she likes what I'm throwin' out."

Bill, Travel Agent, 32

"Men perform according to the way you stroke their ego. So tell him what it's like, meaning, ("I like the way you do that…." or "Right there…. it feels sooo good when you hit it like that…. Or something as simple as, "Please don't stop."*). Men love that shit!"*

Frank, Lab Tech, 57

Sex, Fucking or Making Love

Sex, fucking or making love, it doesn't matter, they're all good. But I prefer fucking and so do most men. What's the difference? I guess you want me to tell you huh?

Sex: Sex is when you just fuck! It's a one-night-stand. Somebody you call just to get your rocks off a.k.a a booty call. When you cum or what's even worse, when he cums and you haven't and the party's over. Sex! Nothing more. Nothing less. Just sex! Most of us would like sex to have a meaning but it just doesn't. This is when we need to get a nut, and it doesn't have to be someone you love or want to have a relationship with. Sex is doing it with someone almost anyone that can make you feel what you want to feel. Having sex is being free to explore every part of you, without having the mindset that it's as bad as we were taught. Sex is impulsive and lacks inhibitions. We need to understand that there is a difference between having sex and understanding sex. Each time we have sex we have a different experience and a different meaning to go along with it. Most times we aren't in the same mood when we engage in a sexual act; therefore one experience may bring about joy and closeness, while another time it may leave a feeling of being empty and worthless. The meaning will then be different.

Now that we know more in this day and age, we also know that sex isn't just limited to intercourse. Any kind of sexual act is considered intercourse. Any moment that we have an experience that brings us closer to another individual is considered intercourse, so we as women know and have experienced an enormous array of sexual reactions and connotations. Girls, with all the shit we can do and play, no experience should ever be the same, hopefully, better. Why try to put extra meaning on something that allows you to be so free? Accept your sexuality and embrace it with all you have, each time you're permitted to share it.

When I'm in a sexual relationship with a man, I get it straight from the beginning what we are to each other. Am I his girl, one of the girls he's dating or a straight up pop off? If I'm his girl, I allow him to experience whatever he desires (excluding other women of course). I refuse to do anything that makes me feel degraded or cause pain to the point of injury. If I'm the girl he sees occasionally, then I introduce him to things slowly. He doesn't need to have his cake and eat it too. Now, if I meet someone I like and we have nothing but a sexual relationship, I would be freaky as hell with him with a little bit of romance (that's good for his ego) and a lot of sexy good times. We don't argue at all.

With sex having no meaning, it means every time you have sex you need to know where you are in that relationship. You're going to have to accept responsibility for what you feel and what you experience. When you're having sex, your mind takes over and whatever you believe you psychologically can make your experience terrifying or put you in a state of nirvana.

There are times when what you like may be very different from the man you're with. Even though his likes may be drastically different from your perspective, it gives you no right to say what they desire is wrong. You have to accept his desires or you can't expect him to accept yours.

Just trust who and what you are sexually. Trust your partner like you'd want him to trust you and trust the sex you have. Enjoy the experience of cumming together over and over again.

I don't know about you women but I feel renewed after a good romp in the hay. I make sure my experiences are full of intimacy, pleasure and a sense of satisfaction on both our parts.

Making Love: Wow! Making love? I remember making love to this guy. He and I had been talking on the phone for almost two years. We had never seen each other in person but we formed a friendship that was out of this world. We talked about everything, and even let each other in on some embarrassing moments. We even shared the hurt that was inflicted on us by someone else. I loved him. I loved him for all his good and bad points. He was my friend, and I loved him unconditionally. Finally I couldn't take it anymore I told him I was coming to New York to visit him. I know he didn't believe me until I got my ticket. I hadn't had sex in over a year and I wanted to lose my new virginity to him. To make a long story short, when he first initiated, it I was nervous and I wasn't totally ready. He caught me by surprise. "Relax," He said as he kissed me gently. "It's okay." He made me feel so good and so comfortable, I gave my whole self to him. While we were making love, he said, "Sonia, this is sooo perfect it's like you're my best friend, my buddy and I love you." From that point on, it was like fuckin' magic, I fell in love with him even more, and I knew I would never forget him. I knew I was making love with him at that moment. During the rest of the trip, we had sex, we fucked a lot and he made love to me often. We fucked at least twenty-five times during my vacation in that week. I couldn't get enough of him when he just turned me over in my sleep and I know we did a lot of fucking.

"I don't have to always have sex to make love. Just being with the woman I'm with, loving her and just spending time with her is sometimes enough for me. If a woman is a good kisser, that alone can feel like making love."

Phil, Plant Manager, 39

"When I make love my primary goal is for her to enjoy it as much as me. We should both be enjoying each other for whom and what we are to each other. When you make love you give yourself completely to each other. "
Dean, Package Designer, 43

"There's plain old sex" He holds up his left hand. *"Then there's making love."* He raises his right hand. *"I'll take making love any day. I know how women want to feel some sort of emotional satisfaction but I like that too. It's like when you fuck and everything is over, you still have something to talk about. If I'm just having sex with a woman and she's physically a ten, but she don't have shit to talk about when we're done," He* laughed. *"I'm sensitive like that."*

Keith, Dentist, 29

"Making love is like being in paradise with the one you love, fulfilling all your fantasies and reaching a state of nirvana."

Mitchell, Physical Therapist, 37

"When you're making love, it's usually with someone you really love and everything is beautiful. It's like you can feel the passion all through your body and you feel like with each stroke you love that person even more."
Jake, Pathologist, 44

Making love, usually happens when it's the first time, or when you're totally in love with every aspect of your mate. Making love happens when you and your man had the worst fight and the two of you miss each other so badly and so much that when you get together it's like fucking magic. The whole feeling is magical and everything almost seems like it's going to be okay.

Fucking: My Favorite! Fucking is a combination of the two, sex and making love. Sometimes, most times you're usually with someone you like, used to go with or a one-night-stand that turned into something more. When you're fucking, it can start off like making love with all the special touching and then the sex that his love tool is working up inside you, makes you just get wild and nasty. You can say almost anything right about now. The exploration, the heat, the breathing, the words, the pounding and then the cumming!!!!! Oh my God, the cumming!!!! When you cum when you're fucking, I'm telling you, it's the best feeling in the world. You're in your favorite position and your pussy is exploding and all you know is, if you had wings you could fly. I love flying and after a good flight and I do mean a very good flight, I laugh 'cause it feels so good.

How's that? Did I feel them out right? Well, those are merely my feelings on sex, fucking and making love. Yours may be different but I betcha they're close.

Adding It All Up

We've come to the conclusion that sex is one of the most enjoyable acts performed between a man and a woman. What's even better is the way the act is carried out, in order to get that feeling we all crave that feels sinfully delicious.

AN EXPERIMENT: The next time you and your man are fucking, after about five minutes, pick a fantasy then close your eyes and start your fantasy. Your man is not to know that you're fantasizing. Afterward, write down what you felt and how it made you feel. Write down what you liked and what you could make better, then share it with your man.

That's when communication comes into play. If you don't have communication, it's like crossing an old, raggedy bridge; it could fall apart at any time. Couples have to let each other know what they like and need in bed or else someone might start creeping. A woman needs more time to get aroused, so you have to let your man know what makes you feel good; how you like to be kissed and where you like to be touched. Let him know how you like your hair stroked, your ass held or your pussy licked. He in return should let you know what he likes and what turns him on. This is also a good time to ask your man how he likes his dick sucked. Ask him if he likes to be fingered or spanked. Does he like rough sex or making love or a little bit of both? At any rate, it's communication time. If you're comfortable about talking about sex it will be a pleasure to perform.

How to Be a Flirt

Let's face it, Women are so much more subtle about flirting that men need to pay close attention to a woman signals. Men aren't used to women flirting with them, and in some cases, they don't have a clue about what the woman is suggesting. Most men I know wish women would make it clear as day about their interest and what they really want. Here are a few ways to help you get better at flirting.

Lesson#1

You're probably going to have to hit him up at least three of four times before he truly gets the message that you're flirting with him. After that, he'll probably make it clear that he's got the message when he smiles or comes very close to you, but he's not going to say anything. By the time he gets the nerve to come over to you, introduce yourself and let him know you're interested and would like to see him again.

Lesson#2

Don't be a woman jerk. If a guy flirts with you and you don't find him attractive, for God's sake be nice. There's always someone watching you and if you're nasty to a shy man, heck, that may limit the possibilities of the one you like to come over. Don't laugh or make crazy faces when he walks away either. At least let him know it was nice meeting him. It's called sugar coating it bitches!!!!!

Lesson#3

Speak softly, or even a whisper. Notice when you whisper, it brings then closer because they want to hear what you have to say. Once you've got his attention, whisper in his ear, "I'd really like to get to know you…. but I'm afraid of rejection."

Lesson#4

Stand-alone sometimes. A friend of mine told me he was afraid to go up to women when they're with their friends. They're afraid they might be rejected. Women seem to have more guts when their friends are around and men are aware of that. So break away from your girls, and help a man work his way to you.

Lesson#5

Let your friends help you out. If there's a guy you like, tell your friends to watch him as you pass by to see if he's looking to take thing a little further. If he looks interested in you, make your move.

Lesson#6

Kick the unwanted men to the curb, but in a nice way. Let them know that what they're saying is not winning them any points. Suggest that he try to be a little subtle and joke with him and send him on his way.

Lesson #7

Be a little daring! Show men what you're working with. You don't have to dress like a whore to get attention. Believe it or not, men prefer their women to have on clothes that are revealing without maximum exposure.

Lesson#8

When you walk past him and he's looking you up and down, his gaze will end on your ass. Look over your shoulder then say "I see you watching my ass." then smile. This lets him know you're playful and interested enough for him to make his move.

Lesson#9

Smile! Smile! Smile! A man loves to see a woman smile. It makes it easier to come over to a happy woman instead of a woman with a screw face (an angry face). Smile, even if your bleeding heart is breaking.

Lesson#10

Flirting is meant to be fun and harmless. Don't put too much pressure on yourself to be the best flirt, a little can and will go a long way. They just need the sign and it's usually a wrap, one way or another.

Kissing

Kissing. Yummy! When was the last time you were kissed? When was the last time you were kissed so deep that your pussy throbbed with excitement and juiced up like a ripe peach ready to be eaten? I know I can kiss, but when a man kisses you like he's in love with you and he sticks that thing in you the way you like it, it's like Gawd damn I love your ass!!! That's kissing and unfortunately, the act of kissing is becoming a dying art. How you kiss a man is an indicator of what kind of lover you could possibly be. It tells him that you're either inexperienced or an old pro. Your kisses can tell him if you like fucking hard or soft or if you like to be playful. Men don't realize the importance of kissing, so it's up to us women to guide them on the right path. We have to let them know that kissing is important and it should be for him as well. Kissing is what gets the fire started. It's the kissing that makes you want to go further and the better the kiss, the further you can go. When the kissing is really hot there is sure to be spontaneous combustion. Show him that kissing brings you closer together, and you want to get inside of him with your tongue. But also let him know that there must be genuine sincerity behind his kiss (or at least fake it 'til it's real). Imagine when someone kisses you and you could tell they didn't want to do it., How did you feel? If you're going to kiss someone, make the kiss mean something. Let him know you don't always have to have his tongue for his kiss to mean something. A kiss on the nose, forehead, the neck, and the ever-loving cheek can say so much. Imagine the neck and the ears, mmm... I once kissed this police officer that I liked from the moment I first saw him. I knew once I got a chance to kiss him, there would be magic. After a long kiss goodbye, he said, "You kiss like you mean it." And I did. We're not together today, but we did a lot of kissing back then. So kiss him whenever you can and mean it! So when he walks away he wants to come back. And he will. He'll want to finish what he started.

How to Improve Your Kissing

1. First of all oral hygiene is very important! No one wants to kiss anyone with bad breath. Have you ever smelt someone's breath on more than one occasion and wonder how their mates let them stick their tongue in their mouth? What You really want to say to them is. "What did you have for lunch? A fresh shit sandwich?"

2. Use your mind. Imagine him kissing you like you're in a love story of your own. Explore his mouth like you were looking for information. But never go deep diving! Sticking (no, ramming!) your tongue down his throat is not a turn on. (You're not trying to find out what he had for lunch.) Hard, darting tongues. Yuck! I dated a guy whose tongue was hard and pointy, I felt like I had an abnormal dick in my mouth.

Of course, this is just a little bit about kissing. I'm sure quite a few of you will do just fine, while a select few will still have a little work to do. Whatever the case, make sure you have a hell of a good time learning how. Remember to take every opportunity to show and express your love a simple little way like a kiss, which often has a big effect. I love kissing; it makes me feel so close to my man.

***Butterfly Kiss**

If you do this correctly you'll feel a fluttering sensation in your heart. With your faces together like you're going to kiss, about a breath away, bat you lashes against his.

***Cheek Kiss**

This is done by gently brush your lips across his cheek. This kiss is rather friendly; it at least lets him know you like him enough to give him a kiss on the cheek.

***Earlobe Kiss**

This is when you gently suck and nibble at the earlobe. Whatever you do don't suck in the inner ear and for God's sake don't do those loud sucking noises. It makes the ear scream and not with excitement. "Whoa!!!! I'm shaking just thinking about it."

***Eskimo Kiss**

Brushing your noses together doing this and is really sweet.

***Eye Kiss**

While he's asleep, very softly kiss the spot between his eyeball and eyebrow bone.

***Finger Kiss**

When the two of you are in a quiet place all cuddled up under an old fashion quilt and you're holding his hand. Bring his hand up to your mouth and seductively suck on his fingers. If done right, it will send a fantastic electric charge straight to his manhood. It's a sexy way to get things started.

***Foot Kiss**

After he's had a shower and is lying back in the bed. Sit at his feet and massage them seductively paying close attention to the base to increase relaxation. While you're looking up at him as you kiss each toe, suck and nibble on them, occasionally licking between his toes before taking the big toe in your mouth. (Demand that those dogs be clean. That means fresh out the shower and into the booties.

***Forehead Kiss**

This is really a friendly kiss or a friendship kiss because you lightly kiss the top of his forehead, it says, "Love you". It has a totally different meaning, if you're having sex. It says I love what you're doing to me.

***French/Soul/English Kiss**

This involves the tongues passionately wrestling with each other.

***Quick-Fast and in a Hurry Kiss**

When you must go quickly; give him a kiss on the nose like a good little boy.

***Suck and Blow Kiss**

While kissing open-mouthed, slightly suck in as if you were sucking the air from your partner's mouth, then lightly blow back into his mouth. If done correctly, it should make you feel a little light headed and your body as though you were floating or lacking oxygen. When you kiss like that make sure you're ready for a little action afterward, there's bound to be a lot of it.

***The Kicker**

Wake him up by tongue kissing his dick. He will be pleasantly surprised.

***Wake Up Mr. West Kiss**

While he's still asleep, quietly lean over kissing his cheek lightly then give him repeated kisses on his cheek until you reach his lips. When he opens his eyes, smile and say. "Wakeup sleepy head. I've got something for you."

What your kiss says to a man.

Lips - If you kiss him on the lips that means you have some sort of love for him, and he isn't that bad.

Neck - Now we all know when you start kissing a man all over his neck, you're giving him every indication that you want him or at least part of him.

Ears - Kissing his ears makes him feel like you're ready to play hide the meat.

Chin - You are so adorable.

Any place else - There are so many things I want to do to you with my tongue.

Places to Kiss

The small of his back
Curve of his waist
Behind his ears
His eyelids
The palm of his hands and Tips of his fingers
The back of his neck
His stomach

The tip of his nose
His lower waist
The top of his feet the area right before his toes
His spine
His collarbone
His navel
His Butt

Foreplay

What is foreplay?

"Foreplay can be a lot of things, but I like to include just about everything. When I'm giving women foreplay, I want the total experience. I know if I give her this pleasure and make her hot like fire. She's all mine. Naturally, we're kissing and hugging then I might start feeling her up then undressing her real slow but just peeling them back. I like the way it feels when we're in the heat and we're trying to get out of our clothes while grasping desperately at each other. Then I'd give her some mind-blowing oral sex. My best friend is a woman and she said that if a man hugs up and kiss the woman they're sexing it makes her relax to the point where the touch of his hands on her skin is so sensitive that she will cum if he fingers her. She said it takes women longer to get stimulated to the point where they want you like yesterday and if I get a woman fully aroused I'll be able to make here cum over and over again."

"Rick, 33, Reporter"

How important is foreplay?

"Since the beginning of time, foreplay was something a man was expected to do to get his woman ready for sex. Most of the women I've fucked always want foreplay, I do it

because I like the way she looks while she's getting hot for me. I'd say it's very important, especially if you want the woman to feel like your sexual encounter was satisfying."

Leo, 62, Supervisor

How do you use foreplay to spice up your sex life?

"Shit! I want the woman I'm with, especially if I like her, to have the maximum amount of pleasure. That requires the proper amount of lubrication and a little time. When I take my time and I know she's at her peak of excitement and she can't control herself any longer. I know I've done my job well and half my battle is over. After that, it's all over for her."

Jack, 27, Teacher

What was your best foreplay experience?

"I don't think I have one really. When I find out what makes her hot I help her to know what I like. I usually like oral stimulation, it gets my dick really hard and if she tells me how much she wants it and how it taste in her mouth, I just get crazy. It increases my confidence level and makes me want to make her glad she came over."

Tom, 21, College student/computer geek

A lot of men are foreplay idiots. They don't know how to give proper foreplay. It's not that they don't want to, they just don't know how, at least some of them. Sometimes we come across men that can make bells ring that aren't even there; thus, bring forth the statement, "You can ring my bell anytime." Then we meet the ones that all they want to do is just jump in and go for the gold. They don't know that the secret to a good night is foreplay and it can make their job much easier and sweeter. You've got to help them learn that you're not going anywhere, and he should take his time. That's where you come in. You need to be very sensuous and sensitive in order to make him feel really relaxed and enjoy foreplay like he never had before. Let him know he's free to do what he likes. Let your body come alive in his hands and watch him get hotter. The two of you must give foreplay for at least twenty minutes to a half hour before he can even think of entering you. You have to help him learn that it's not how hard he pumps that makes a difference to a woman, but it's the foreplay that has been received that makes a partner feel not only loved and special, but most of all desired. If the two of you build up the feeling slowly, making every part of your body ache with pleasure, then you can fuck him hard. At this point the two of you will be so lost in each other's love, you'll both probably cum together. That, as we all know, can be very powerful. So be his teacher and take him through "Fundamentals of Foreplay 101". Once he learns how to please you with his hands and mouth, it will become a regular thing. You'll find he'll want to make sure you twist and turn under his hands all the time. While you're turning him on and letting him have his way, he'll be fucking you making you cum until you cry for him to stop. And you know that will never happen. We women can get really greedy, if it's a good dick

Oral Pleasures

Every man is different in what he likes; from the type of woman he sexes to the woman he marries. But when it comes to dick sucking, they're all the same. Bring it on!!!!! The thought and feel of a woman sucking, licking, kissing and loving a man's penis can do more for the male ego than ten women coming on to him at the same time. It's a turn on. He can picture all the things in his mind that he'd like to say and do to you and he will. In his mind you will be his slave, his whore, a princess who thinks she's too good for him, but loves sucking his dick without end.

Even if you're a little shy about it, you won't be for long. He's going to get you so turned on; it's going to make you even hotter for him. With all that heat, there's bound to be a night of pure fire. For some women, the drive to give oral pleasures is always there. For some, it is and will need to be acquired. At first, it will be the man initiating the act but as you develop a passion for it, you'll find that you'll be the one taking hold. Believe me, sometimes you'll feel so damn horny you shouldn't be the least bit surprised if you find yourself cumming while you're sucking him off. At that moment, you'd do just about anything to make him feel good. And yes, you'll be able to tell the difference. You'll hear the difference in his moans and groans and that'll make you lick him and suck him all over. It's not all the time that I feel like a wild woman. Sometimes I don't want to even look at a dick, let alone suck it, but if you want to make and keep him happy sometimes you gotta do what you gotta do.

One of my friends told me that she was giving her man oral pleasures and the feeling she got while sucking him nearly put her over the edge. He knew she wanted to give him all the pleasure she could possibly give. That really excited him, knowing that she cared for him that much that she'd take him in her mouth. One thing I must caution you about and that's to beware of the drippy dicks. I don't know about you but a drippy dick turns me way the fuck off. I know some men have drippy dicks, but damn!

"I love the feel of a woman's warm, wet mouth. I feel like I'm coming in from the cold."
Spongie, 25, Printer

"I like my dick to be sucked every chance I can get it sucked. I like to watch her head bob up and down on my dick and it disappears into her mouth. I like the feeling I get when she looks up at me with those eyes. (He laughs) Those dick-sucking eyes. I just love my dick being sucked. I like my dick being sucked as well as making her feel good. I don't like a woman to feel bad or like I don't feel the same about her. I like her to feel good and I want her to feel good when she's going down on me. I like the level of intimacy we reach and the beautiful sensation it brings."
George, 33, Barber

"When a woman is sucking mi wood (a Jamaican term for dick), the feeling is just like wow!"
Dennis, 40, Restaurant Owner

Fellatio
A.K.A Sobbing on the knob! Choke the chicken! Or more Commonly known as dick sucking

Like everything else, there are many different techniques to "dick sucking" and just as many positions. I'll blow off a few (pardon the pun) and you can pick or try as many as you like. Well, we all know the basic. Him lying on his back, legs spread apart and dick waiting to be brought to life or he can sit with you between his legs while on your knees. The one I think men prefer the most is when he's standing and you're on your knees like you're begging to suck his dick. As you're sucking him, he'll place his hands on his hips with that hellified master grin on his face. Don't feel intimidated. Little does he know you're in control and he's about to get it! A lot of women don't like this position because it makes them feel like a whore. To hell with that!!! It's just the two of you, so girl you better kneel before your man and his dick and suck his dick like you're trying to suck the chrome off a bumper.

My favorite is laying side-by-side, head to toe, facing each other. Ahhhhhh. Yes! Sixty-nine!!! I don't think there is anything better then my man eating my pussy with his big hot lips and me sucking his magnificent dick. Once I really get into it I like to lie on my back with him on top of me and he's fucking my throat. I like to feel the excitement of him in my mouth while he's humping. Then I just really relax and let him go as deep as I can take it without gagging. Surprisingly, the more turned on you are the deeper you're willing to let him go. But be careful here, in this position you have less control on how deep he goes.

"I feel my eye roll back up in my head and my mouth is open and I feel like my breath is being taken away. I keep fucking her mouth and if she takes it all and let me cum in her mouth, I go crazy!!! I love it and it makes me want to fuck the shit out of her and make her feel like I'm feeling. That shit does something' to my mind."

Craig, 53, Retired

Unfortunately, oral sex is considered taboo. Everybody's doing it but no one wants to talk about it. Up until 1986, 18 states (Washington D.C., Alabama, Arizona, Virginia, Florida, Utah, Idaho, Rhode Island, Kansas, Oregon, Louisiana, Oklahoma, Massachusetts, North and South Carolina, Minnesota, Georgia and Mississippi) couldn't legally engage in oral sex. It was considered a low-life sex act and was against the law. Some people are embarrassed to let someone know that they bury their face in someone else's private parts. Some women are embarrassed by the gagging or choking they experience, no need to be alarmed ladies, it's natural. A little gagging happens to the best of us. Sometimes it could be the smell of your partner's natural odor, the smell of the sexual fluids or just the thought of a dick in your throat. When anything touches that part of your throat that's not used to being touched it produces a gagging effect. It's like that feeling you get when you go to the dentist and he sticks that stick in your mouth to hold down your tongue, only he goes back a little too far. Remember how you gagged the first time and laughed? Laugh when you gag on his dick, it'll make the whole experience not so bad.

I remember one night when my husband and I went to a party. I had 4 1/2 glasses of champagne and I was totally fucked up. When we got home, we were doing our thang and I was giving him oral pleasures. Well, all hell broke loose when a little too much saliva was in my mouth. With my state of mind, all I could think about was babies in my throat. I started gagging. "Give me the garbage can." I said between gags. I threw up and every time I thought about those babies, I threw up some more. He was rubbing my back and saying. "It's ok." I shrugged his hands off my shoulder and yelled. "Did you cum in my mouth?" Of course, he answered. "No. I swear." I thought about it again and threw up what was left of what I thought were babies. Call me Mrs. Spits not Mrs. Swallows.

How to Suck a Dick

Kiss and nibble about his body. Kiss him, embrace him, and make him feel relaxed and loved. Nibble kiss in and around his ears working your way down his neck trying to cover every inch of his anatomy with your tongue. If there's a certain direction or area he wants you to pay close attention to, he'll more than likely guide you in that direction. But there are a few men that will let you do it on your own so they can see what you're working with. Suck his nipples and keep working south. When you're finally at your destination, start kissing his inner thighs and upper part of his legs playing close attention to the area that separates the thigh and the torso, until you begin to see life. Kiss and lick his balls and moan while taking him in your mouth. And hum. Humming has a vibrating effect that produces a unique pleasure. The dick and balls can be sensitive to the touch, but the perineum (that area between the balls and the anus) is the runner-up, and its favorite part of a woman's body is her tongue. As you're taking him in your mouth lick and kiss the head until it becomes intense, then lick the underside where the main vein is. Make sure your moves are somewhat smooth and effortless and not too jerky. You want him to feel as if you know exactly what you're doing. Take his dick in your hands while sucking, and gently apply a little pressure and keep sucking, kissing and licking him until he grows big and hard in your mouth. Using the musical motion of thrusting in and out, grab his ass and pull him in close to you and take him as deep as you can. You won't be able to go that deep if you're not real good at it because you might start gagging with that big piece of flesh in your throat. His dick will become harder and you'll find yourself getting more excited and start moving and sucking like you're a pro. Because he's going to be fucking your mouth like a pussy, so to speak, you will need to keep some control. Wrap one hand around the base of his shaft while you're sucking to prevent him from going too deep, or at least deeper than you want. The more you want to take in, you just, unwrap one finger at a time until you've reached the desired and most comfortable length in your mouth. Once you're comfortable with everything, ask him how he likes it and does he want it harder or softer, faster or slower. Me, I really love to talk. After I'm used to and comfortable with my partner, I want to talk dirty. Sometimes I like to be nasty and hardcore; it really turns me on. Then there are the times when I'm quiet and relaxed. You may think you can't do this, but you can and will. Don't be offended if you hear him say, "Suck my dick", He's now caught up in the moment and he's yours for the taking.

Just keep sucking and licking his dick, every once in a while jacking him off a little to move it on a little faster. Take him back in your mouth and suck him until he climaxes. If you love the taste of cum, you can let him cum in your mouth but if you're like me, I bring him to the point of climaxing and just when he's ready to release, I jack him off until he's finished cumming. Then I, in a sexy way, wipe away the cum and finish sucking him until he's hard again and let him fuck the shit out of me any way he likes.

ALERT!!!!! One thing that pisses me off is a man that likes his dick sucked, but he can't do the same to you. Yes you will give him a bligh a time or two because you really like him or he's your mate and you love him. But!!!! If he thinks he's too good to give you oral pleasures, he might have to be put in the limited category. At this point, you only do this when you want to. If he goes someplace else to get it… so be it. Your body is just as good as his. You won't be able to stop a man from being a cheat. What you do after he does go outside looking is totally in your control. You only have to take so much shit of the feeling that he's scorning you. For those of you that love to suck dick, carry on as usual. Now let's move on to orgasms.

(Sneak-Tip) This Jamaican guy told me; a lot of women in Jamaica give the man, *seasoned breast.* I Was like, what? The man say, "Mi no nyam pussy" Without the man knowing, the women stick their finger in their hole and rub their pussy juice on their nipples and let the man lick it off. He may no go down like a bowcat but he just ate pussy on some seasoned breast.

Orgasms

Oh, that feeling!!! That wonderful, magical, free flight, head so light, body free feeling. I want some more of that feeling. I can't imagine anyone going through life without ever experiencing that excitement. Unfortunately, it's mostly women that can't seem to get that, primarily because the men always seem to cum when we're this close. Does this sound familiar "Yes right there. Oooh, that feels so good. Please keep it right there..." Then you feel him tense up. You know he's cumming. He makes those funny animal sounds and his body begins to buck releasing the rest of that funky feeling. Yeah, that's the feelin' you were trying to achieve. "Did you cum?"

He lets out that satisfied laugh. Yeah, you know, that one that you share when you both cum. "Yeah. You?"

'Hell no!!!!!' You say to yourself. *'I told you I was right there you inconsiderate motherfucker. You know I wanted to cum! You knew I needed this as much as you! I'm so fucking angry with you I could cut off your dick! Almost' kiss him on the cheek.* "It's okay." You lied! Why? Because you didn't want to hurt his feelings or make him feel less of a man. But if he were someone you didn't care about too much, you just want to be fucked; you'd let him have it.

Orgasm, such a small word for such a big experience and everyone's experience are different. Orgasms are sexually released tension. The more tense you are, the stronger the orgasm. We all know everyone wants to cum.

It's not the primary reason for having sex but it's running a close second. There's always the closeness it brings, the beautiful laughter you experience after you've had a great cum together and that's the whole idea. But you shouldn't think about it that way. You should be concentrating on making your man feel good as well as yourself. Cumming together is not a necessity. It's a luxury. If you slow down and watch him cum, you'll get an overpowering ego boost that can turn you on more than you'll ever know. When you concentrate on having an orgasm, it produces anxiety, which can bring about problems making love and making it a terrifying ordeal. So make it light and fun. Enjoy yourself with him and make him fly with pleasure. What you need to know is men experience the same feeling as a heroin user when they get high. They can achieve this sensation alone, but for a better bang, they need a partner. The release of prolactin will cut off his drive for sex for almost an hour. In most cases, he could be ready anywhere from minutes to hours. In some rare cases, some men are able to get it up in minutes, that's because they release less prolactin when having an orgasm. I think I met a couple of them.

More Tips 'cause I need more words

1. Relax and take it easy, you've got all the time in the world.

You don't have to be in a hurry. There's nothing worse then rushed sex (unless you're having a quickie). It's not fulfilling and it usually leaves your partner feeling somewhat used. Women take a little longer to get aroused than men and it takes us longer to cum, so make sure you have the proper amount of foreplay. A good thirty to forty-five minutes of straight fucking will usually be enough for a man. That means pace yourself so you'll reach your orgasm, and you'll both arrive at your destination at the same time.

2. Discover

There's nothing better than getting to know your lover's body. Let yourself experience the madness of exploration. Your bodies deserve to receive pleasure. Find out those little areas that make your body quiver and shake. A man loves when a woman takes the time to find out what makes him and his body perform at its peak. Hint: The tongue is usually an excellent tool in exploration. The warmth and tenderness of the human tongue is a mind blow in experience.

3. Be Sporadic

Many times you might not be on the same page when it comes to making time for love making or fucking. If you have kids, life-changing crises, or you are just tired, you might not want to have sex and that can affect the way you feel and perform. But don't worry too much about that. Everyone's off at one time or another. Just make sure that the time you are together, you experience as much as possible, and you make him cum. If he knows you're tired, all he needs is to bust that nut and he'll do that and fall asleep. Who knows, maybe by the time he puts it in and works it a little, you may get aroused and be ready for another round.

4. **Don't bring your problems to bed.**

As we women know, if there are problems going on outside the bedroom, it can affect they way you feel and your performance. When the rent is due and the gas & electric is about to be shut off, the last thing we're thinking about is sex. Men don't think that way. They feel that if you got a roof and some food, everything is fine and there's no reason that there shouldn't be any fucking. Believe it or not, they expect you to know and understand that when it's time to fuck, it time to fuck. No questions asked. The best thing to do it try to limit the stress in your life, and take care of important issues outside the bed room or when sex is not on either of your minds.

5. **Go on dates with each other.**

Once a week make a date with each other, and you don't have to wait for him to make the plans. Do things you did when you first got together, those were the things that you liked about each other. We get so caught up in our everyday life and all the responsibilities that we forget to live and love each other the way we did when we first met. So take and make that time to be alone together. That means, if you have kids, get rid of them! (At least for the night.)

6. Games anyone?

Play some quick card games where you can wage certain parts of your body to be revealed or touched should you be the loser: you can even take turns living out fantasies, the winner gets to pick. If you're not too creative, go to one of your local adult stores and they should have plenty of things for you.

7. Go on long rides

Every once in a while, go on a long ride together. Play some soothing music with no words or his favorite mellow CD. Don't forget music you like; it'll make the ride more enjoyable. During this ride, you'll talk and flirt with each other. You might even find a spot off from traffic and go at it like two teenagers. Whatever you do, just enjoy the ride.

8. Read! Read! Read!

No matter how good we think we are, we can always learn something else. Just like you picked up this book, pick up another one and learn something new to knock his socks off. Shoooooooot! You're going to have to learn hundreds of ways to keep him turned on, if you plan on being with him for the rest of your life.

What Do Men Want From Women

1. Men want a fun and excitement!

When a man goes outside of a relationship, he's searching for that fun and excitement that he used to have with you. With the other woman, there are no problems, just fun loving unadulterated sex. Of course, there are going to be times when reality steps its ugly head in and you have to deal with it, but try hard not to make the problems in your life make you a bore.

2. Men want sex anytime they feel the need.

Men get turned on by different things than a woman does. He can get turned on with you in rollers and a pair of panties. Women are attached to men emotionally and we want to feel like no other woman matters. A man wants his woman to be a bit of a whore in the bedroom. If a woman can freak her man in bed she will get more of what she wants from him. Hopefully a faithful and dedicated lover. Being more vocal, and having the attitude along with it, is more likely to get a freak in return. This is where creativity comes in; thus solidifying the process of bonding and emotional attachment. Men get closer to their women through physical contact and when we make love or fuck them as often as possible, we're showing them how much we love them. When we don't give our man sex, he's not feeling the love so to speak. Men seem to relate better with the act of being physical, because, when he releases his juices, he feels so connected.

3. Men want women that cook.

I know. I know. But look at it like this. Don't you like your man to cook for you? Well, men are ten times worse. They love women to cook their meals. That's that momma thing again. If you can fuck them, feed them and let them watch sports. Your job is half done. So learn how to cook! Hint: Men love fried chicken. So work on it. Start with wings if you don't have a clue.

4. Men want you to support them and boost their confidence (ego).

Girls, men are babies and they have to be pampered in certain ways. They need to hear, " I believe in you You can do anything you put your heart to." or "You can do it, baby!" They like you to ask questions about their job, and how was their day. They don't like to be put down or made to feel less than a man.

5. Men want you to look great.

They like their women to be nice looking with bodies that look like they work on them night and day. Looking great does not mean you have to look like America's next top model. Men like their women to look a certain way not only in public but they like her to be nice looking at home. Simply by watching your weight (Even you like your man to look good), take time out to work on your body, not only for him but for yourself as well. If you feel and look good to you, you'll feel a lot better about displaying it to him. If you don't feel good about your body and you try to cover it up from him, you'll send out negative thoughts and he may read this as you're not finding him attractive. Men love women that are confident and sexy. It seems to turn them on when a woman knows what she wants and what she is able to do. Look at Beyoncé. She's got men black and white falling out over her, why? Because she's sexy as fuck and the men dig that shit like crazy. So spice up yourself and look good as often as possible. When other men find you sexy and confident, your man will take notice and step up his game too.

6. Men want you to respect and understand them

Men want to be treated with respect, even though some don't deserve it. When we give love and respect while being kind and understanding, most time we get that back. But if you disrespect you man and make him feel useless, you get negative feedback, and that can ruin a good relationship and destroy a bad one. Therefore respect is very important to men and woman. Treat each other with love and respect and it'll help make a better relationship.

7. Leave them alone

As you know, when we get home we like to have a little time to just relax and ease our minds. Men need that too. Just give him a hug and a kiss and let him have his space to unwind from the day's events. In return, that will be your time to do something for yourself or with the kids. After you've left him alone for a while, he'll come looking for you. Give him a nice welcome kiss and you'll feel yourselves connecting on a fresh level. Make sure your kiss means something, like, "I love you." "Welcome back." Or "I'm ready to fuck if you are." So, make sure you practice your kissing together as often as possible. Hint: Men like to know you have a life other than them, but they also want you to be there, when they need you.

8. Fantasies

We all have them. It could be, being swept off your feet by a knight in shining armor or being sexually assaulted in the best way by a stranger. You could have thoughts about your brother-in-law or your best friend's husband. We all want something done to us that someone else might think is nasty or freaky as hell. Live out your fantasies and make your sex life come alive. Ever notice how men always say when they cheat, "You didn't want to do the things I wanted to do." Or "You're always at work." Or "You don't want to try anything different." Men need a variety and they say variety is the spice of life. So spice that shit up. Throw some new shit on him and make him feel like he's got an undercover freak. He may even wonder if you're cheating cause you're turning his ass out. When I fantasize, I do and say things I wouldn't normally say. I love talking dirty and talking dirty turns most men on, along with a little ass in their face.

9. Communication

I can't tell you how very important communication is. It's the key to any successful relationship. You have to tell your partner what it is that you like and in return you need to know what he desires. It's very important that you let each other know what you're thinking and feeling. Unless you're both good at mind reading, you won't have a clue at keeping them happy.

Tidbits - What Men Want in Bed

"Believe it or not, sometimes I just want a good night's sleep!"

James, 27, Accountant

"Everybody is different. Since everyone is different, let me just say men need and want the same as women, we need someone who we can communicate with and express our true desires. Both have to have some sort of mutual priorities and desires in order to keep the relationship at a cohesive level. Keep things flexible and always, always (he stresses) keep the level of trust up at all times. So many men and women do wrong things in and out of bed, but the thing they do the most is the failure to communicate with each other."

Lawrence, 48, Supervisor

"I want her to be my own private little whore. I want her to let me do whatever I want. It doesn't matter if she sucks my dick or let me fuck her in the ass. I want what I want when I want it".

Alec, 35, Teacher

"I want passion! I want to feel like my woman wants me as much as I want her. I want my body to come alive with the feeling of her treating me like a king. I want

her to be there mind body and soul, not on the bills or across town. I want her to be herself and flow free."

Clark, 23, Artist

"Be honest, truthful and Passionate... If I'm doing a good job let me know. Show me how good I make you feel. Don't be afraid to show me what you want or what you want me to do or how I can help you enjoy it more. Without being rude or acting like the man, move my hand and show me how to rub you then let me do my thang."

Ty, 45, Bouncer

First of all, Ms. Sonia, I love your title. I'd like my woman to read this book, then fuck me like there's no tomorrow. If she cares for me and enjoys being with me, and she makes me feel it. I'll take her places she's never been. Concentrating on me and not too hard on your technique as long as you're there and making me feel good, you're doing everything right."

Shawn, 33, Bar Owner

"Women don't come with a manual, and they certainly don't have any instruction ...and every one of you is different. So, you have to let us know when something feels good when something doesn't. Just make sure you move your hips the way we like then whisper sweet nothings like, "Yes! Fuck me just like that." "Yes, just like that."

.JJ, 30, Police officer

"There are times when I want it faster, slower, harder, softer, longer, and sometimes I just want her to do

me. I'm easy to please, and what I don't know and you want, I can be taught."

Brandon, 28, Chief

"I don't want to hear "no" or anything that sounds like it. If a woman can't be open-minded to what I want we have a problem. As long as I'm not hurting or degrading her she should be down with it. I don't want to feel like I can't be myself around her. If I can't be myself in the bedroom, I'll lose interest."

Ruben, 25, Computer Operator

"I don't want a woman who is one type of person when we're dating and then a different person when we're married."

Ron, 36, Graphic Artist (newly married)

69 Ways to Turn Him On

1. Play with yourself while he's on the way home. When he walks in, let him see you playing with yourself. If he wasn't in the mood on the way home, he will be once he gets a load of you and your sweet but naughty little sex act.

2. Have a friend take pictures of you in various positions and have them sent by a special deliverer to the office, followed by a phone call letting him know what you want him to do from there. You can either meet him for lunch or you can be lunch. Just make him want to get with you by any means necessary.

3. Put a tape recorder in the room while the two of you are fucking, without him knowing. When the two of you are relaxed and laying back turn on the tape and watch his surprise and the turn on. If he thought he was through, he'd better think again. It's funny how turned on they get when they hear themselves fucking, especially if you're carrying on like he's the best you've ever had, without sounding phony, and you want him to do this all night long.

4. Let's make a note of that! Notes will do it every time. Slip a little note in his lunch, in his shoes or even the sun visor. Whenever he finds the note, it will be a sweet surprise. He won't get it wrong because you'll say exactly what it is that you feel or are trying to say.

5. Call him at work and let him know what's waiting at home for him. Then give him an example over the phone. Don't forget to moan and groan. Give him all you got then hang up the phone, when you're just about to cum. If you find it hard to talk to him over the phone without him fucking you, get a dildo and fuck yourself well before you call him. When you feel like you're at the point where you can get fucked and go, call him talking dirty. Fuck yourself and hang up when you're about to cum.

6. When you're having dinner at his mother's house, whisper in his ear, "I don't have any panties on." Dart your tongue in and out his ear enough to make him shiver with delight. Then look in his mom's direction and tell her how juicy the meat is. What will his mom think of that?

7. Take the kids to mom and set up for the date. When he comes in, have on your waitress lingerie. Let him know you're here to serve him in every way possible. If he needs his balls licked, you're there to serve. If he wants you to massage his entire body with your tongue, you're there to serve. And serve is what you shall do.

8. When you know he's going to have a big meeting, put a pair of your panties in his briefcase along with a note telling him what you're going to do to him when he gets home, and then do it! (Make sure your panties have your pussy or natural body scent on them. They always smell the panties. Wherever they are, they just have to smell the seat.

9. Before lovemaking or when you're ready for round two. Tell him one of your fantasies in detail; if he's timid

give him some nasty encouragement. The kinkier he is the deeper the fantasy can be in order to get a better response.

10. Have him tell you his fantasies and make one of them come true. Everybody has a little freak in them, so if you just relax and let it flow, you'll find that freak in you. That could be in a restaurant, his mother's house, the car, the expressway and anywhere else that makes your blood boil. It's not that you want someone else to see you; it's just the thrill and the thought of being caught. It's just like an affair. You don't want your mate to catch you, but it's the thought of doing something wrong that makes it feels so damn good. It makes the moment hot, passionate and freaky.

11. Fuck him to him in a fast food restaurant. The men's bathroom is the best. It has less traffic. Get it as good as you can while making as little noise as possible.

12. Make tapes of his favorite music that set his mood. After that, concentrate on giving him total pleasure.

13. Make sure wherever you are, the room smells good. Lightly spray the perfume he likes best on you, on your sheets, the towels he uses and anywhere he lays his head. Then make it the beat night of his life. Whenever he smells that scent, it will remind him of that night. TIP!!!! Spray a light bulb with the perfume he likes. Let the bulb dry completely. Later when the light is in use, the scent will linger on.

14. Treat him like a king. Gather in a nice pretty, sexy dish filled with fruits to feed him. Also have some

champagne, cheese, and crackers. After you feed him the cheese and crackers, let him sip the champagne from the goblet you're holding. For dessert, place the fruits in and about different parts of your body and tell him, "These are the forbidden fruits and it's time to taste the nectar of the gods.

15. Mirrors! Mirrors! Mirrors! There's nothing better than watching yourself fuck! Imagine him fucking you, the fuck is feeling so damn good you could scream bloody murder, and it would still feel good to you. Then you just happen to catch a glimpse and a good look at what he doing to you. You tell him to look in the mirror while he's fucking you, and to say whatever comes to his mind. He'll get so turned on, he'll work even harder making the out come better for both of you.

16. Never bring your lover to a messy bedroom or a messy house for that matter. Your sheets should be clean and fresh, and please don't forget the pillowcases. Your bed should make him want to just run and jump in. He should feel free and able to breathe in deep if his face is in your pillow.

17. Be prepared! There's nothing worse than being in the mood and you have to run around looking for condoms, sex toys or anything else that should just flow.

What you will need:

a) Condoms (a must for a peace of mind)
b) Body oils, lotions, and lubricants
c) 2 small towels. One wet and one dry.
d) Tissue (to wrap condoms in)

e) Toys! Toys! Toys! Nothing like an extra penis when your man needs a break. Bring them out, it will improve relations.

f) _______________

g)_______________

h)_______________

18. Before he leaves for work tell him lunch is going to be delivered. At lunchtime show up with a picnic basket for two with everything you need. Wear an easy to remove dress with no underwear on. Feed him lunch with you as dessert.

19. Go out for an evening at your favorite dance club. Let him know you've got something for him while feeling him up. Then tell him you need him right then and there. Find an empty stall or an area in the club you can almost be alone. Turn around back ways and let him go for what he knows. If you're really daring, leave the stall door open and give the rest of the men the show of their lives. Once done, take your man out and dance the night away. There's more pleasure waiting after the nights done.

20. Go for a long drive then stop on the thruway, and serve him up with an express pass.

21. Freak him by licking the crack of his ass, while massaging his dick. (Do not stick your tongue in the opening) Tease him and watch how willing he is to have something soft stuck up his ass. He'll start rolling around like a woman in heat with his lips almost begging you to fuck his ass with your tongue. If he's really relaxed and

open, he'll let you put your finger in his ass and pretend you're fucking him.

22. Bathe him. Fill the tub with water as warm as he can stand it with lots of bubbles. Sensuously wash him all over with a sponge. Make sure his favorite drink is on the side of the tub, the candles are lit and your perfume is all over the shower curtains. Love music is playing in the background and you're talking to him, kissing him and letting him know it's all about him while making promises of oral pleasure and a night of blissful sex.

23. Give him a massage that's too good to be true, paying close attention to his ass. Men love to have their ass massaged.

24. Talk dirty to him. If it's new to the both of you, you might be a little nervous and feel funny at first. Don't feel bad; it's a natural feeling. If the two of you just relax, talking dirty is only telling what your true feelings are when it comes to sex. Everyone likes to talk dirty, even if it's in his or her minds. You ever fuck a new guy and he's fucking you so good you want to let him know but you think he might think you're a freak or a whore? But that's what they want to hear. He wants to know that his dick is making you react like this. They feel so hot and horny that you got to let him know as graphic as possible.

25. Vibration stimulates. There are different types of vibrators on the market with different speeds but serve the same purpose. Massage his body with the vibrator taking care not to neglect his dick and balls. Then watch him

scream and squirm. Make sure you use slow sensuous movements while making a skin-to-skin connection.

26. Once things are really hot and you know what you can get away with and what he'll tolerate. Use a vibrating dildo (with lubricant) and run it across his body and if he's really open, massage the opening of his ass. At first, he might jump and say no, but assure him you will go only as far as he allows you to go. Assure him that you can make this moment sweeter, then all he has to do is relax and enjoy the moments.

27. While you're giving his oral pleasures, grab his ass with both hands and squeeze and massage him the way you like it. The combination of both of them will drive him wild. Just when he thinks he can't get any higher, slowly and very, very slowly and very, very, very, very slow for a macho man, begin to finger the opening of his ass and watch him nearly pass out. Nibble at him, suck him, bite him and do anything that makes him cry out in pleasure.

28. Mananna -split. Lay, him flat on the bed. Take some softened ice cream and spread it on his body. Top it off with bananas, cherries, whip cream and your favorite syrup. Make sure his dick area has the most of everything. That's when it really becomes a treat.

29. After a soothing shower or bath, dry him off with your tongue, then say, "Coffee, tea or me?"

30. Put some ice cream in your mouth and suck his hard throbbing dick.

31. Take a single (red) Popsicle and began to masturbate (Not in your va-jay-jay) while he's watching and jerking himself off. Share the Popsicle and fuck like there's no tomorrow.

32. Give him a splendid bath and clean him off good. Light up the candles to scent and light the room. Turn on the sexy music and massage him to the point where he's almost falling asleep. Then kiss all over his body until he becomes aroused. Masturbate in front of him while letting him know exactly what's waiting and in store for him.

33. If he comes home like clockwork, take a fresh shower, before you begin and sweeten yourself up. Five minutes before he walks in, or if you're easily excited, run and jump on the bed and begin to finger yourself. If you know he's in the house, call out his name while you're moaning and groaning. Saying, "Fuck me (his name). I miss you baby! I just want to feel you inside me." The next thing you know, he's either going to watch or he's going to be fucking you quicker than you know.

34. Take some eatable, erotic oil and lube up your lips. Then let him slide his big dick in and out of your mouth.

35. Get a massage vibrator with different attachments and massage him. For extra smoothness use a massage oil to make it glide along his body. Use the different attachments to give him different pleasures. There's an attachment to make every part of the body feel good. It's also important that your free hand has contact with his body

at all times. As long as you maintain that skin-to-skin connection at all times, there will still be that feeling of love. Don't be rough with his body. Do all the things you'd want him to do to you. You know where his sensitive spot and parts are. Love them and take special care of them.

36. Some men are apt to try new things. While you're giving him oral pleasures, lubricate your fingers and finger his ass. For extra pleasure, use a cock ring. They're usually found at your local adult bookstore in all different sizes. The cock ring fits snug around the base of the cock and helps keep his dick harder and bigger longer.

37. Each of you writes down five things that you'd like done to you, separately, on a piece of paper. Fold then in half and drop them in a bag. Take turns picking one out of the bag. Once you pick out of the bag you must do whatever the paper says to your partner. Remember you might pull your own paper, so make sure whatever you put in the bag; you're willing to do. No, if, and or buts about it. Happy pickings!!!!

38. Have him tie you up and do whatever he likes. Then tie him to the bed and ripe him apart.

39. Play out last. See who can last the longest. The first one to cum has to pay off the bet. The two of you agree on what the bet will be, then fuck each other like wild lost lovers, and see who the winner will be.

40. Play strip! There are so many games on the market that are fast and simple to play. It's like playing strip poker.

If you lose you have to take off a piece of clothing. (Socks count as one). This game is better when you're getting to know each other. Once you get to know each other, you can have different acts performed on you for no more than three minutes at a time.

41. Strip dance for him. All men like to see you slithering and acting like a stripper. Get your favorite body moving music; because you know you're going to be doing' some serious fuckin' when that strip scene is over. Make sure all the music is fuck music. Began taking off your clothes as you dance, displaying the inclination of sexual approval. Next give him a lap dance, either facing him or with your back to him, and ride baby ride. If you want to feel like you're in a real club, have him stick dollar bills in your lingerie.

42. For one day, get rid of the kids and the two of you stay completely naked, preferably in a hotel so you don't have to worry about the mess you make. Just do a lot of caressing, kissing and spontaneous hugs, until you both can't take it anymore. But whatever you do, fuck! Make those loud noises you always wanted to make. Let that be your "freaknique".

43. Ask him to masturbate while he is blindfolded. When he's masturbating, lick his body. He's not allowed to touch you, just his dick. You, on the other hand, can touch whatever you want.

44. While you're having friends over for dinner, the music is playing and everyone else is talking, slip off to the bathroom for a quickie. Once you're made him cum, clean

yourselves up quickly, but real sexy. Get dressed before him, give him a kiss and say, “After you get yourself together, cum join me in general population and I’ll let you know how I’m going to suck your dick later.” Then walk out and close the door.

45. When you’re giving him a good hand job, caress and pull down gently in a good rhythmic motion while applying a little pressure. Keep it going until you feel him fucking your hand. At that point, keep stroking, massaging and kissing him passionately as you can, with a little bit of animalism. He’ll think his ass is falling in love with an angelic whore. When he grabs at you, quickly and smoothly, sit down on his dick and fuck him until he cums. When he cums, keeping riding, him until he begs you to stop, but never stop.

46. Forbidden fantasies - Dress up like a man (yes with a mustache) and ride around with him. Talk to him letting him know what under your trousers. See who gets the most looks while you’re driving.

47. Give him a full body massage using only your body. Warm up some body oil and pour it on his body then climb on top of him and swash your body all over his.

48. Have a midnight picnic on the living room floor. Have cheese and crackers along with some fruit and wine

49. Make a pussycat trail leading from the door up the stairs, to the bathroom with the tub full of water, and glow in the dark objects. Use your body wash to bathe him.

Rinse him and towel him dry. (Remember he's not to lift a finger

50. While he's asleep, wake him up the best way possible, and that's by using your mouth. You can't wake up two birds at one time by taking him into your warm mouth, and seductively suck until he wakes up smiling or fucking, whichever comes first.

51. Dress sexy every now and then for no reason at all. Just get sexy for him. If your looking sexy does something for him, and his dick happens to get hard, don't be afraid to throw that pussy on him.

52. Sometimes he just wants to fuck! You could be bending over changing a baby's dirty diaper, and he'll want to run up in you. Just let him bend you over and have what it is he really wants, and that's a quickie.

53. Set up a night where the two of you are relaxed. Make sure you have on something cute and sexy. Have all his favorite snacks and drinks. Then let him pick out a porno movie from the collection you've been picking up on the sneak tip. (HINT: Men like the two-woman thang!)

54. Let him tie you to the bed. Once tied let him playfully whip you with one of those whips you get from the adult toy and variety store. They're not painful and can be a much-needed change. Now if it's pain you want, they have a whip for that too.

55. Some men like to pretend they're rapping their girl. No lovie-dovie shit. It's like a real rape scene. No physical

or mental harm should occur. You just let him fuck you hard and in any position. It's a lot more fun than you think. I like when he pulls my hair hard.

56. Some men are hopeless romantics. They love to pamper their women and shocking, as it may seem, even the toughest man like a woman to be romantic with him. Take him out to dinner then a movie. Afterward take a long romantic drive to the beach. When you get home, just cuddle up with him. (That's unless he desires a little more.)

57. Be open and want to communicate. Find out what he likes and what turns him on. Men find it sexy when a woman wants to know all she needs to do to make him happy, in and out of bed.

58. On a movie night put in one of the most romantic movies ever made, (Pretty Woman). I'll make the toughest man smile, and want to make his woman feel special. In return, you'll most likely reap the benefits, 'cause turn on ignites turn on.

59. Now this one makes me say humm… A guy told me he was really freaked by a woman he was fucking. She started sucking his dick and fucking his big toe at the same time. He said it felt so good he was floored.

60. Send him some flowers on a Wednesday for no reason in particular. Make sure the roses are white. It's a symbol of friendship and these flowers are for your special friend and lover.

61. Have a candle lit dinner (at a table) but you both are naked and you're not allowed to touch pussy, breast or dicks until dinner is done.

62. Take a shower together, and after you're clean give each other a second shower using your tongues. (No soap please!!!)

63. Show up at his place or pick him up from work with nothing on except a trench coat. On the ride home, ride with your coat open and let him play with your pussy on the way home.

64. Read to him. Get an erotic or XXX book and read the story to him, while you're in bed sipping wine or your favorite drink. As the story comes to a climax, you two will be next in line.

65. Cook dinner and set the table while in the nude. Sit him down and let him relax, then parade around him, until something pops up. He can either eat dinner or dessert first.

66. If he's an eater, put him in the torture seat, by sitting him down facing you. Cock your leg up on the side of his thigh, lean in and let him visit the candy shop.

67. Voyeurism: Do you like being watched? Do you like taking a chance on being caught? Go some place that's busy, but not too secluded and fuck each other's brains out. If you're treating him, give him the best road job he's ever had.

68. Next time you're at a party sneak off to them bathroom and fuck him until he cums like a water faucet. You'll find that you'll enjoy the party or gathering you're at a lot more once you both bust a nut.

69. Take this book, a bottle of Jack Daniels (or your favorite liquor) and read this book together. Experiment and lose your fucking minds. Here's a good time to experience the 69 position.

Happy Fucking!!!

POSITION

Well, this is something I really like to talk about, positions. There are so many, I don't see how people get bored. Just to show you how bored we get, look at how many time you change positions in a single session. We crave change and we desire excitement and demand results. Now. Imagine men. They are sooo physical when it comes to sex. They love to look at their dicks going in our va-jay-jay or the way our asses and assholes just sits up high. It makes them want to stand up in it and give it to us in the worst way. In the changing of each position, he's usually like us looking for a position that will help us get it all. Notice when you're in the doggy style position, he's losing his mind and the more you head to the head down ass up position, the deeper he goes and the better it feels. In this position, you both get what you want.

All positions might not be stimulating for both partners, but there are advantages to a lot of them and as you some disadvantages. Like one position might feel good to you and give you time to rest, while your partner might feel little pleasure and is getting tired. Another position that might feel perfect to him might be very difficult for you physically. When you find the positions that you both like, and want to blend them in together for unique level of passion, this is where the give and take come in.

I'm going to start with the most common positions. It's the one we all start out with our first time, making up and just plain old lazy. There will probably be some you've tried and some you've never heard of, or they might just go by another name. At any rate, I'm sure you'll get a lot of pleasure out of some of these. If you're the type that's not so open, you will be after some of these positions. Your man will be wondering where you been hiding that nasty little sweet bitch. Here goes something'!

Missionary - This is your first-time position. The woman lies on her back with her legs spread and her knees raised, and her partner lies on top between her legs the man has direct penetration. The missionary position is the most popular lovemaking position of all, because it allows body contact and good deep penetration. The lovers can kiss and hold each other at the same time. From this position, the woman can move to wrap her legs around her lover's back, or you can close them tightly underneath him, while he spreads his legs apart.

Butterfly position - the woman is lying on her back, the man is standing and he lifts her pelvis to gain entry.

Deckchair - The woman is on the bottom, lying on her back she pulls her legs up and opens like a V. The man is on top holding her legs up. This is very good for deep penetration, the further he pushes her legs back the deeper he can go. He has a lot of control here.

Missionary on the side - The woman is lying on her side the man kneels down and enters her from behind. This one is good when you're mad at him and you want to get a nut. You can fuck his dick with your legs tight together while he's tearing that ass up. You won't have to look at him and you'll both get what you want. WARNING!!! This position can and will lead to more sex.

Doggy Style - The woman is on all fours facing down and the man enters from behind.

Face Down Ass Up - This is just like doggy style only the woman torso is much lower and her ass just sits up like, fuck this pussy! This is one of the man's favorite positions. It's also one of the most natural one for us. In the FDAU position, the angle of the woman vagina and the curve of the man's penis fits perfectly and cause the right amount of friction. Shit! I love this position to death! Sometimes I feel real nasty, and I want it hard and deep. I like the way he looks and feels in control when he's pounding into me.

"I love holding on to her hips slamming my dick into her while pulling her back hard. She lets out these cries like it hurts but she doesn't want me to stop."
Ian, 33, Player

"I like to look at my dick going in and out of her pussy and I like the way a woman's asshole looks like it's talking to me when I'm fucking her. If I hold her by the hips and ass and ride that shit like a fuckin animal. Maaaaan! " **Oscar, 45, Store Owner**

Spider position - In this rear entry position the woman is lying face down, legs open wide and the man is lying on top. With your legs spread and him supporting himself and his weight on his arms. By raising your ass slightly or by putting a pillow under your hips to aid in lifting you, you can have even deeper penetration She spreads her legs and he supports his weight on his arms. If she raises her bottom off the bed slightly, perhaps with the aid of a pillow under her hips, then it will be possible to achieve deeper penetration.

Foot Pon Shoulder - The woman is lying on her back, legs on his shoulders and her feet locked behind his neck. This position is sooooo good when you're making up. You get his entire dick and you can kiss him so deeply this way. And ladies don't worry a little alcohol and some good dick will make you fold like a pretzel every time.

Riding Cowgirl - The man is lying on his back and the woman is on top facing him. Simulate riding a horse with your own twist. This position allows the man to rest. For some extra excitement, I tell him to hold on to my hips tight and fuck me. After a while, you'll both get his rhythm that's out of this world! Fucking has never felt so good.

Astride - The man is lying on his back on the bed and the woman sits astride him, that way she can control their pace. With the woman facing the man she can squat, kneel and use her hands for support. She can also kiss and caress or lay her body on his to increase intimacy. For deeper penetration, try doing it with the woman facing away from the man.

Riding Cowgirl in Reverse - Man and woman are in the same positions as riding cowgirl only the woman is FACING AWAY from the man. In this position, you can play with his genitals, ball, nuts (what-ever you want to call them) and his ass, if he gets down like that.

Spooning - The man and woman is laying side-by-side facing in the same direction. The man enters from behind. This is good when you both want to fuck, but you're just a little tired. It's nice to fall asleep like two spoons. The 'spoon' position is so named, because of the close fit of the two bodies.

Crawl - This is a deep penetration position where the woman is on all four and the man in kneeling behind her. This is a great position, if you're really horny and you want your body touched. The man and woman are able to thrust against each other and the man has access to the woman's butt, clitoris, and breast. You can also do this position standing up with the woman supporting herself against a table or chair.

Crusade - The man and woman are both lying on their backs sided by side. The woman lifts the leg closest to the man. If you get tired you can rest your leg on his body. The man enters the woman from under the raised thigh and crosses the leg that's closest to her over her body. This position can be sooooo intimate, because you're able to kiss and hold one another.

Cunnilingus - In cunnilingus, the man stimulates his partner's vulva and clitoris with his lips and tongue. For most women, cunnilingus gives the most delicious sensual pleasure, and it is the best way of climaxing. It is also extremely arousing for her partner.

Fellatio - In fellatio, the woman sucks, licks, kisses, and strokes her partner's penis. Exquisitely satisfying for the man. Fellatio can also give enormous erotic pleasure to the woman, as she senses his responses, and his total abandonment to her.

Prop Top - The woman in lying on her back with about two to three pillows under her butt to lift her up. The man kneels down between her legs giving her oral pleasures; he can open her legs as far as he needs them to go. Once stimulated, he can penetrate her while supporting himself on his knees. He holds on to her legs and has the control to pull her into him as he thrust. I can only imagine how you'll enjoy this. The way your body will be angled, will make you wonder why you never tried this before.

Head to toe - Both the man and the woman are lying on their backs with their legs in different directions. Her legs are spread apart across his legs. He enters her giving her control. You can hold on-to each other's legs to intensify the sensation and to move closer.

Cumasittra - It's the same as the position above, except that the man and woman are sitting, and the legs are behind each other's butts. This position is so sexual.

Lap Dance - The man sits on a comfortable sofa with the woman facing him straddling his lap. She moves up and down on him with her arms wrapped around his neck, while supporting herself with her knees. Here girls, you have all the control, you decide how fast or slow you want to go. If you prefer deeper penetration, you can turn around with you back to him.

Armchair - In just like watching the football game or *Being Mary Jane.* The woman sits in an arm-chair, then the man kneels in front of her and enters.

Split-level - The man kneels between the woman's legs with her lying on her back and her legs wrapped around his waist. You're gonna love it 'cause he can lift your legs over his shoulders, stimulate your private parts or just lay down on you and love you. He has total domination, and if he bends forward with your legs on his shoulders, he can go deeper and the kissing will make you feel so sexy.

Lumber Jack- Standing up with the woman against the wall, the man picks her up and enters her using the wall as support. The woman's legs are wrapped around the man's waist and her arms are around his neck.

Quickie - The woman bends over supporting herself on anything that's available. The man enters her from behind, but I guess you guys already did this before.

Black bee - The man sits on the floor or on the bed with his hands behind him. The woman sits on top with her hands on his shoulders or arms wrapped around his neck.

Advance Black Bee - This is the same as the black bee, except that the woman's legs and hands are on the man's shoulders.

Playing the violin - The woman is lying on her back, with her ankles on the man's shoulders, and the man enters from behind

Sitting on the toilet - The man is lying on his back, upside down with his knees bent. He almost look like a toilet. The woman sits on the man and bounces up and down.

Persuading of the piper - The woman is lying on her back with her ankles on each of the man's shoulders. The man kneels in front of her and slides his dick down in her.

The proposal - The woman kneels in front of the man with her legs apart. The man kneels with one knee on the floor. It looks as though he's proposing. He penetrates but this one is no good if his dick is short. (I'm jus' sayin'.)

Drilling for oil - The woman is on her shoulders with her back up against the wall, the couch or the headboard. (Pretend you're doing a headstand only you're on your shoulders). Her legs are folded like an Indian. The man gets on top of her vagina and fucks her in a standing position.

Riding the Steer - The man lies on his back, and the woman sits on his penis. Using the support of his knees, she lifts herself up and down. He helps controls and steadies her with his hands on her butt.

69 - Is the position both men and women alike are feeling' each other. You can be side by side. Man on top or woman on top. You can lie and be any way you want, as long as you're both getting it at the same-damn-time.

Horizontal reverse - The man is lying on his back. The woman is on top with her back to him. She's facing down with her torso as low as it could go.

Rocking chair - The Man is on bottom, and the woman is on her back, on top of the man facing up.

Special K - The man and woman lie on their backs, heads pointing away from each other. Each places one leg on the other's shoulder (using it for a brace) and the other leg out somewhat to the side ,so that they form a K.

To the T - The woman is lying on her back with her knees up and apart. The man lays on his side, perpendicular to her, with his hips under the arch or her legs.

Anal Sex

Wow! There's so much to talk about when it comes to anal sex and, why men like it so much. Today it is used as another method of lovemaking, instead of the everyday shit. Anal is something completely different. Why is something so good such a taboo? First of all, there are so many nerve endings in the anus. Having said that, with pleasure, comes pain. Well, although there is an immeasurable amount of pleasure, the initial feeling is pain. When you're attempting this, you should learn to relax and know that your partner is there for pleasure. You will soon be taken over by this pleasure.

What's the best way to enjoy anal sex?

"RELAX!!! RELAX!!! RELAX!!!! I can't stress that enough!!! Don't just jump into it 'cause there's something about that pain that makes your toes curl. The sphincter muscle is the muscle around the anus and that muscle won't let a thing get through unless it's totally relaxed. Start small, then work your way up to something bigger. Once you're tried the finger or plug a few times you're then ready to move up to bigger things. There can be so many things"

Why do men want anal sex?

"I don't like one over the other. But I love ass. It the way it feels inside the tightness damn! Everything! I love

me some spice and if a little booty will keep our sex life spicy. I'm all for it."

Wilson, 28, Real Estate Agent

"I think those are all rather "impulsive reasons" and well, I would argue not based on very many facts or realities."

Jay, 40, Business Owner

A version of spooning or me lying with my back on his chest, is one of my favorites for this position, as he can play with my breasts and clitoris. That way I can guide the thrusts. I enjoy spooning because you also get to feel his hands roaming over different parts of your body.

Of all the many other positions, anal sex is a treat that can be very enjoyable to both partners. Anal sex can be very stimulating and exciting. When the two partners really enjoy each other the act can be very warm and tender. Patience is also a quality a man needs to possess. I suggest, for the first few times that you don't even consider doggy-style. Girrrrrl, Your toes will lock with and unusual cramp your asshole will yell...Help Me! LMAO! Mind you, the woman only feels this pain or person the penis is being inserted into. May I suggest the spooning position or the woman lying flat on her stomach. Anal sex has been around every since people started having sex or every since the caveman days. (They just didn't talk about it.) It's simply another experience to try. For example, I'm sure there are females on this board who were/are curious about giving head? In the same respect, guys who haven't had anal sex with a female are curious about it. Now it is possible that anal sex feels different than a vagina. I don't believe it makes a man gay if he wants to have anal sex or like having anal sex. What makes a person gay has nothing to do with sex. It's simply that they are attracted and want to be with a person of the same sex. Anal sex is something that some men want to try and some don't. The same goes with women some are open to the idea and others who aren't. I also don't believe that having anal sex with a woman is a way to dominate her. If she agrees to it then how is that any kind of domination? People like to explore things sexually. There are things out there that people are into far beyond anal sex.

Audra, 24, Exotic Dance

The Questionnaire

1. Do you like a man/woman to make the first move?

2. Do you like a man/woman to play hard to get?

3. What turns you on in a man/woman?

4. What turns you on?

5. Are you sensitive? In what way?

6. Do you have to have more than one man/woman in your life at a time? Why? Is it a man/woman thing?

7. Which one do you prefer most? Sex, making love or having you back blown out? Why?

8. How do you feel about one-night-stands? Will you respect him/her tomorrow?

9. What sexual acts do you like performed on you?

10. Are you freaky, in what way? What freaky things do you do?

11. Have you ever had your ass licked? Did you like or dislike it? What did it feel like?

12. Have you ever had anal sex? Did you like it? What about it did you like or dislike? Would you do it again?

13. Do you like to use sex toys? Which is your favorite?

14. Do you like porn movies? Do they turn you on? What do you like about them?

15. Do you masturbate? How often? What do you fantasize about when you do?

16. Do you like to watch a man/woman masturbate?

17. Do you like to be whipped or spanked? How does it make you feel?

18. What can a man/woman do to turn you on?

19. What's the longest amount of time you've had sex in one session, without a break?

20. Do you like your mate to wake you up with oral sex?

21. Do you like to play rape scenes?

22. Do you like bondage?

23. Do you like role-playing? Who's your favorite person to play?

24. What are some things you look for in a man/woman?

25. What do you think about marriage?

26. What's your definition of a good relationship?

27. What is your idea of a romantic evening?

28. What characteristic do you like and dislike in a man/woman?

29. What's your best get back together story?

30. What do you like least about sex?

31. Do you practice safe sex? If no, why not?

32. Do you remember your first kiss? Describe it.

33. Where's the weirdest place you've had sex?

34. What's the strangest thing you've been asked to do in bed?

35. Describe what it feels like when you cum.

36. What's the hardest part about being a man/woman

37. What's the best advice you can give a man/woman on keeping his woman/men happy?

38. What your favorite fantasy that you'd like to come true?

39. Should a relationship end over bad sex? Why?

40. Have you ever performed oral sex? Did you like it?

41. How do you know when you're in love?

42. If your man/woman is in the mood for sex and you want to sleep, what would you do? Why?

43. What makes a woman/man sexy to you?

44. Are you having an affair now? Why?

45. What would make you cheat? Why?

46. What's your favorite position?

47. What's the most romantic movie you've seen?

48. What do men/woman really want women/men to know?

49. If there were one thing you wanted a woman/man to know about sex what would it be?

50. Tell me what you think about sex, relationships, cheating and anything else you think a man/woman should know about a woman/man.

Remember

HAVE FUN AND BE RESPONSIBLE
USE PROTECTION!!!

AUTHOR'S BIO

Sonia Calloway is a graduate of The College at Brockport State University of New York, majored in Communication. Have been a freelancer writer, newsletter editor, greeting card designer and dollhouse maker. She lives in Rochester, NY. 69 Ways to Turn Him On, In and Out of Bed. Her first book, has been called "A promising debut" "Funny, entertaining and engrossing" by a panel of readers. My Sister's Killer, a mystery novel (Coming in 2017) will surely be a page-turner.

www.ingramcontent.com/pod-product-compliance
Lightning Source LLC
Chambersburg PA
CBHW071641050426
42443CB00026B/803

* 9 7 8 0 6 9 2 8 7 2 6 3 5 *